Ships and Seafarers

Rosemary Rees
Sue Styles
Adam Hook

HEINEMANN

Heinemann Library
a division of Heinemann Publishers
(Oxford) Ltd
Halley Court, Jordan Hill, Oxford OX2 8EJ

OXFORD LONDON EDINBURGH MADRID
ATHENS BOLOGNA PARIS MELBOURNE
SYDNEY AUCKLAND SINGAPORE TOKYO
IBADAN NAIROBI HARARE GABORONE
PORTSMOUTH NH (USA)

First published 1993

98 97 96 95 94 93
10 9 8 7 6 5 4 3 2 1

**British Library Cataloguing in publication
data** is available from the British Library on
request.

ISBN 0 431 07500 X

Designed by Ron Kamen, Green Door Design
Ltd, Basingstoke, Hants
Printed in Spain by Mateu Cromo

Acknowledgements

The authors and publisher would like to thank
the following for permission to reproduce
photographs:

Arxiu MAS: 4.2C
Barnaby's Picture Library: 7H
British Library: 1B, 8.1A
British Library/Bridgeman Art Library: 7F
Trustees of the British Museum: 1A, 2C
J. Allan Cash Photo Library: 7I
Peter Clayton: 2B
Dagli Orti: 7D
C. M. Dixon: 3.1A, 3.2A
Mary Evans Picture Library: 4.9A, 5.1A, 5.2B
Sonia Halliday Photographs: 4.1A
Michael Holford: 2A, 7E
Imperial War Museum: 5.3A
© Jamie Lawson-Johnston/Pickthall Picture
Library: 5.5B
By Permission of the Master and Fellows,
Magdelene College, Cambridge: 4.4A
Mansell Collection: 4.5D
Mary Rose Trust: 4.4C
© Max/Pickthall Picture Library: 5.5A
© Mirror Group Newspapers: 5.3C
National Maritime Museum, London: 4.1B,
4.5A, 4.7D
The Board of Trustees of the National Museums
and Galleries on Merseyside (Merseyside
Maritime Museum): 5.2A
National Portrait Gallery: 8.1B
Peter Newark Pictures: 4.6A
Racal: 7J
The Sutcliffe Gallery, Whitby: 6A, D, E, F, G, H, I,
L, M, N, O and P
Syndication International: 4.4B, 4.4D
Ronald Toms/Ace Photo Agency: 6J
© University Museum of National Antiquities,
Oslo, Norway: 3.2B
By courtesy of the Board of Trustees of the
Victoria and Albert Museum: The Viking Ship
Museum, Denmark: 7C, 8.2C
Adam Woolfit/Robert Harding Picture Library:
4.4E, F and G, 4.7A
Zefa: 5.4 A and B, 7G

Cover photograph: The cover illustration shows
the *Argo* being equipped. From a 15th-century
manuscript in the Bodleian Library, Oxford.

Thanks are also due to Random Century
Publishers (The Bodley Head) for permission to
reproduce Source 8.1C, taken from *Pugwash and
the Fancy-Dress Party* by John Ryan; Cambridge
University Press for Source 4.2A, taken from *The
First Ships round the World* by Walter Brownlee.

Every effort has been made to contact copyright
holders of material reproduced in this book. Any
omissions will be rectified in subsequent
printings if notice is given to the publisher.

CONTENTS

1 The first boats

Ten thousand years ago, when people wanted to catch fish from the middle of a river, they sat on a log and floated out to where the fish were. Sometimes they paddled with their hands. Sometimes they used wooden paddles, or poles to push the log along. However, single logs rolled over in the water. Anybody sitting or standing on a log ran the risk of being tipped off. But logs tied together into a **raft** floated well. Rafts were more useful than single logs. A raft could carry more than one person. So one person could paddle and steer while another fished. Rafts could carry people and goods across rivers and even seas.

Source
A

People made rafts from bundles of reeds, driftwood or logs. Anything would do, as long as it floated. This carving was made about 2,600 years ago. The fisherman is balancing on an animal skin which has been filled with air so that it will float on water.

The fisherman comes from the ancient land of Assyria. He is probably fishing in the River Tigris. The River Tigris flows through modern Iraq. Assyria was in the north of modern Iraq.

One of the problems with rafts was that they did not keep water out. No matter how tightly the logs were lashed together, water seeped up in between them. Anybody travelling on a raft was bound to get wet, and so were any goods they had with them. People thought of a new way to use logs. They used their stone axes to hollow them out. Sometimes, if the wood was very hard, they burned a hollow out of the log. They made a hollow big enough for one or more people to sit in the log. These were the very first **canoes**. They were made about 8,000 years ago.

People used the materials they found around them to make canoes. The Australian **aborigines** made canoes out of tree bark. First they sewed pieces of eucalyptus tree bark together to make the skin of the canoe. Then they pushed a wooden frame inside the skin to keep the sides apart. The Indians in North America made canoes in the same way. They usually used birch bark. Canoes like this were watertight and light enough to carry easily.

This aborigine painting shows a man fishing. He is standing in a bark canoe.

Kon-Tiki

In 1937 a Norwegian called Thor Heyerdahl went with his wife to live for a year on some islands in the Pacific Ocean. They wanted to find out about the way of life of the people who lived there. What they discovered reminded them of the way of life of people who lived many years ago in Peru, long before the Incas.

In 1947 Thor Heyerdahl and five friends built a raft made from large balsa wood logs lashed together. On the raft they built a small cabin for sleeping in, and for sheltering from the weather. The raft had a mast and a large, square sail. They called it the *Kon-Tiki*. They sailed from Callao, in Peru, to Tuamotu Island in the South Pacific. The distance they sailed was 4,300 nautical miles, and the voyage took 101 days. This showed that it might have been possible for people, long ago, to have made the voyage.

2 Ancient Egyptian and Greek ships

The first boats used by the Egyptians were probably made out of bundles of **papyrus** reeds, lashed together. The Egyptians used papyrus boats for fishing and for ferrying goods and people up and down the River Nile.

Source A

This painting of an Egyptian ship was made in about 1400 BC.

In about 3000 BC the Egyptians began to build wooden ships with square sails and oars. They used sails when the wind would blow them in the right direction, and oars when there was no wind or the wind was blowing the wrong way. These ships meant that Egyptian merchants could leave the River Nile and travel by sea to trade with countries like Palestine and Syria. They also sailed through the Red Sea and down the west coast of Africa.

Source B

These are models of papyrus fishing boats. They were put in the tomb of a wealthy Egyptian nobleman, Meket-Re. He lived in Thebes and died in 2000 BC. They were discovered in 1920 by an American archaeologist.

This picture of a Greek warship was painted in 510 BC. It is painted on a vase.

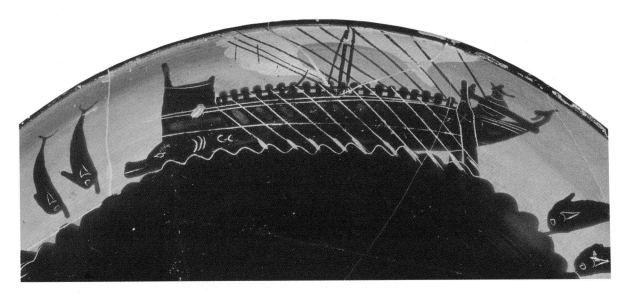

The ancient Greeks, too, built ships with square sails and oars. They used them for trading and for war. Some of these **galleys** were huge, with rows of oars, one above the other. They were rowed by slaves. It took 1,800 slaves to row the biggest galleys.

Square sails were used on ships in the Mediterranean Sea for thousands of years. Look at the pictures of the Egyptian and Greek square sailed ships (Sources A and C). You will see that the sail hung from a huge **spar** which was attached to the mast high up. The spar and sails could be swung round using the ropes at the bottom of the sail. This meant sailors could move the sail to catch more of the wind. Sailors steered the ship with the large oar at the back (**stern**) of the ship.

Papyrus

A great number of different sorts of reed grew along the banks of the River Nile in Egypt and in marshy ground there. One of the most common reeds was the papyrus. Its official, Latin, name is *Cyperus Papyrus*, but most people call it the Paper Reed.

The ancient Egyptians made a sort of paper from these reeds. They put thin slices of the stem side by side, then another layer on top and sometimes a third layer on top of that. They then pressed the papyrus together hard, and soaked the whole lot in water. After a few days the Egyptians took the soggy 'paper' out of the water and dried it. They used it to write on.

The ancient Greeks and Romans used papyrus to write on, too. You can see ancient papyrus manuscripts in the British Museum in London.

The Battle of Salamis, 480 BC

One of the very first sea battles we know about is the Battle of Salamis. We know about it because a Greek historian, Herodotus, who was about four years old when it happened, wrote about it years afterwards. So did the Greek poet Aeschylus, who took part in it.

The Persians wanted to destroy the Greeks. A great Persian fleet waited off the coast of Greece. Ahead of them was a narrow **strait** between the island of Salamis and mainland Greece. Somewhere in the strait was the small Greek navy. Persian ships blocked the sea channel on the other side of Salamis. The Greeks could not escape. On the cliffs the Persian King Xerxes watched and waited.

Themistocles, the Greek leader, ordered a single line of Greek galleys to row out of the straits towards the Persians. Three battle lines of Persian warships moved forward to meet them. Suddenly the Greek galleys reversed oars and rowed back into the straits. The Persian ships followed – into a trap. Greek galleys were waiting for them. They rammed and smashed the Persian ships. Then Greek **hoplite** soldiers jumped on board and massacred the Persians. King Xerxes watched in horror as his fleet was destroyed. His dream of conquering Greece was over.

Source D A modern painting of the Battle of Salamis.

8

The sea vanished
Under a clogged carpet of
    shipwrecks,
limbs, bodies,
No sea, and the beaches were
cluttered with dead.

**Part of the poem written by
Aeschylus about the Battle
of Salamis.**

Themistocles

Themistocles lived and worked in Athens between 523 and 458 BC. He was a soldier and a statesman. He managed to convince the Athenians that they needed a strong fleet. After the Battle of Salamis he insisted that the walls of Athens were built higher and stronger than ever before.

How did things change?

The ship in Source A on page 6 was built in about 1400 BC. The ship in Source C was painted about 510 BC, and was built a short time beforehand.

Both ships had sails and both ships had oars. Now think about what was different between them.

3.1 Roman trading ships

Source A

This is a picture of a Roman ship that carried corn. It was painted on a wall in Ostia, a port near Rome, around AD 200. The ship was called *Isis Giminiana* and the captain's name was Farnaces.

The Roman Empire brought peace to the lands around the Mediterranean Sea. This meant that these were good times for trade. Most goods were carried by ships, which kept as close to land as they could so they would not get lost on the open sea. They usually sailed between March and October to avoid winter storms. Even so, many Roman ships were wrecked.

Roman ships carried goods, or **cargo**, from all parts of the Empire to Rome. They carried goods like oil and honey from Greece, corn from Egypt, figs and fishpaste from Spain, cloth from Gaul (France) and tin from Britain. Roman ships carried food, weapons, clothes and money to Roman soldiers wherever they were in the Empire. They carried goods to sell in the cities of the Empire, too. For example, Roman ships brought glass, wine, fine pottery and jewellery to Britain.

Source B

The merchant who overloads his ship must be mad. He piles on the cargo, then sets sail, even when a storm is blowing up. Why does he do it? For money, of course. But before the night is over, the poor fool finds himself in the water, with his purse in his teeth. His ship and cargo are lost.

Written by Juvenal, a Roman poet, in about AD 150.

A map of the sea routes used by Roman trading ships between about 27 BC and AD 410.

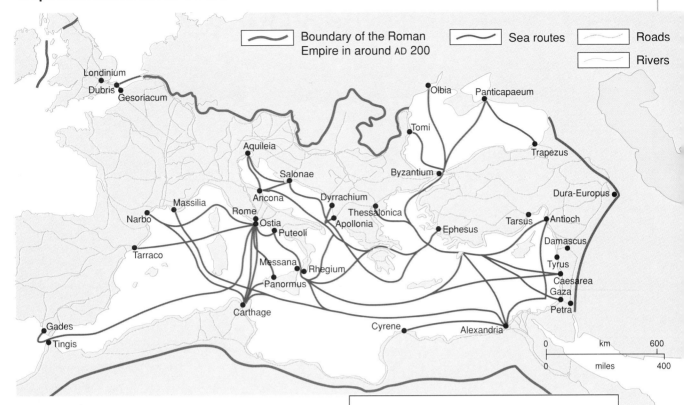

⌇	Boundary of the Roman Empire in around AD 200	⌇	Sea routes
		⌇	Roads
		⌇	Rivers

Ostia

Ostia was a large port on the River Tiber downstream from Rome. It was at its busiest in the 2nd century AD when trade flourished in the Roman Empire. More and more people went to live in Ostia because there was plenty of work in the docks. The Romans built high-rise tenement blocks to house all the people.

Here are some examples of the time it took the Romans to travel between these sea ports:

Journey times

Carthage – Narbo	5 days
Ostia – Tarraco	6 days
Ostia – Gades	9 days
Alexandria – Cyrene	6 days

They built squares, offices and public buildings. They built shipping offices around the *Piazzale delle Corporazioni*, a large square in the centre of Ostia. The offices were decorated with beautiful murals of sea scenes. People working for Roman and overseas trading companies worked there.

The ship in Source A is called the *Isis Giminiana*. It was really a river boat. In the painting it is being loaded with grain in Ostia, and is getting ready to sail up the River Tiber to Rome. The grain probably came from Egypt, a country which exported a lot of corn to Rome at this time. You can see the captain, Farnaces, holding the rudder in the stern of the boat. The men walking up the gang-plank, carrying sacks of corn, are porters. Many different sorts of people from Rome and Ostia found work in the docks.

3.2 Viking explorers

The Vikings were great explorers. They wanted to find new land to settle on; they wanted to trade, and they wanted to raid. Between about AD 700 and 1100 they sailed up rivers deep into Germany, France and Russia. They reached Kiev, Istanbul and Baghdad. They crossed the North Sea to Britain. They sailed to Iceland and then on to Greenland. In about 990 they reached America, which they called Vinland.

The Vikings were able to travel so far because of the ships they built. Viking ships were made out of wood. They were long, slim and light, and had oars as well as sails. Because they were light the ships could be sailed in shallow water and carried between rivers. They could land on beaches and river banks. Viking ships were strong enough to survive storms and did not break up in rough seas.

Source A

This Viking stone was put up by a woman called Estrid in memory of her husband. The writing says 'He visited Jerusalem and died in Greece'.

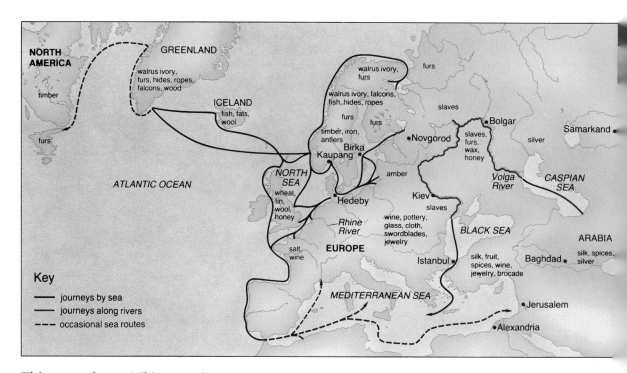

This map shows Viking trade routes. It shows where they explored by river and sea, the places they went to and the goods they traded.

Viking leaders and warriors were sometimes buried in their ships when they died. We know a lot about Viking ships because archaeologists have dug some of them up. This Viking ship was excavated at Gokstad in Norway, in 1880.

How did things change?

On this page you can see an excavated Viking boat, and on page 10 you can see a Roman boat. Were Viking and Roman boats very alike, or not alike at all?

In this Unit there is a map of Viking trade routes and on page 11 there is a map of Roman trade routes. Did the Vikings and the Romans trade in different places or the same places?

Was this because they traded with the same sorts of goods, or different goods? Or was it because their ships enabled them to make the same sorts of journeys, or different journeys?

Eric the Red

Eric the Red was a Norwegian sailor who lived in the 10th century. He sailed west from Norway and explored the coast of Greenland. He encouraged other Vikings to sail to Greenland and establish settlements there.

Leif Eriksson

Leif Eriksson was Eric the Red's son. He, too, crossed the North Sea and landed in 'Vinland'. Many people think this was America.

4.1 Lateen sails and caravels

A thousand years ago Arab traders sailed in the Mediterranean Sea, the Red Sea, the Persian Gulf and the Indian Ocean. They carried goods like rubies, silk, sandalwood, spices and slaves. Their ships had deep **hulls** to carry cargo. The Arabs did not use square sails like the ships of the Romans and Vikings. Square sails worked well when the wind was blowing in the right direction. However, they were difficult to move round if the wind was blowing from the wrong direction, and could make the ship tip over. The Arabs used sails which were shaped like a triangle. These were easy to turn in any direction to catch the wind and sail the ship in the right direction. They were called **lateen sails**.

This picture of Arab traders was painted in 1200s.

Source A

14

Henry the Navigator (1394–1460) was a Portuguese prince. He wanted Portuguese sailors to explore the coast of Africa and discover a route to the Spice Islands and China. He set up a school of navigation and paid for expeditions. The first expeditions were made in ships with square sails. Then Henry's ship designers built a new type of ship with lateen sails. It was called a **caravel**. It was easy to manoeuvre, and light enough to row. Caravels were ideal for exploring the coast of Africa.

In 1492 **Christopher Columbus** crossed the Atlantic Ocean. He had three ships: the *Pinta*, the *Nina* and the *Santa Maria*. The *Pinta* and the *Nina* were both caravels, but each had a large square sail as well as the lateen sails. Many ships' captains began mixing lateen and square sails.

Columbus

When Christopher Columbus was young, sailors who wanted to reach the Spice Islands in the East Indies travelled east. Columbus worked out that he could reach the Indies by sailing west, across the Atlantic Ocean. He had not, however, worked out the distances properly. When his ships reached America, Columbus was convinced that he had reached the Indies. He never believed otherwise.

rce B

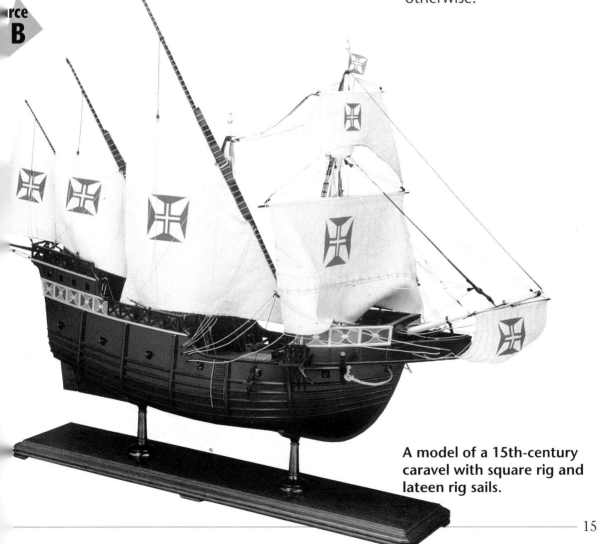

A model of a 15th-century caravel with square rig and lateen rig sails.

4.2 Magellan's journey round the world

No one knows for sure what Magellan's ships were like. By looking at pictures and plans of other ships which were sailing the seas at the same time, historians have been able to work out what Magellan's ship might have looked like. It would have looked something like this drawing.

He did not tell them everything about the plans for the voyage, because his men might, in amazement and fright, refuse to go with him on so long a voyage.

This was written by Antonio de Pigafetta. He went round the world with Magellan, and wrote down things he saw and did.

On 20 September 1519 five ships sailed down the river from Seville to the sea. Their sailors thought they were going to make a routine journey across the Atlantic to America. However, their Captain, **Ferdinand Magellan**, planned to go further. He wanted to get to the Spice Islands in the East Indies by sailing west. No one had done this before. The usual way was to sail east. He planned to sail south, following the coast of South America. He hoped he would find a way through to the Pacific Ocean.

It took Magellan 38 days to get through the narrow straits at the southern tip of South America. One ship was wrecked; another turned for home. Three ships got through to the Pacific Ocean. It was emptier and larger than any of the sailors had ever imagined. They ran out of food and water. Many got **scurvy**; some died. Magellan himself was killed by people who lived on one of the islands he visited. His crew later burned one of the ships because there weren't enough people left to sail it. At last, in November 1520, the two remaining ships reached the Spice Islands. There the ships' holds were crammed with spices. They left for Spain. Soon one of the ships began to leak badly and had to turn back.

This picture of Seville was painted in the 1500s.

In September 1522 a battered ship moored in Seville. It was the *Victoria*, the only ship left from Magellan's expedition. Five ships with 234 men had set out; only 18 men and one ship returned. They were the very first to sail right round the world.

Quarrels

Between 1492 and 1530 Spanish and Portuguese sailors discovered new lands. The Portuguese and Spanish governments quarrelled about who owned these lands. In 1493 Pope Alexander divided the unknown world between them. Later, Pope Leo X was so pleased with an elephant given to him by the Portuguese that he said they could have any land they reached by sailing east. Neither government was happy with this, and they sent expeditions to race each other to the richest lands.

4.3 Life on board ship: the 1500s

Life was hard for sailors 500 years ago. Most of them worked and slept on the open deck. They were burned by the sun, soaked by the sea and rain, and frozen by the winds. Sailors usually had one hot meal a day, which was cooked on deck. Food and drink was stored in the hold of the ship, along with ropes, sails and firewood. Fresh food soon went bad, so the sailors ate that first. Rats and maggots usually got to the rest. The sailors drank water, or water mixed with wine. On long voyages the water went foul and the wine turned to vinegar.

Sailors hardly ever changed their clothes or their boots. Most of them had tiny **lice** crawling over their bodies. They got terrible diseases and many of them died. The disease they got most often was scurvy. No one knew how to prevent it or how to cure it.

A ship like the one in Source B could be sailed by about 30 men. The captain divided them into two **watches**. Each watch worked for four hours and then rested for four hours. It was the job of the **ship's boy** to keep an eye on the **sand glass**, which measured the time. He had to call out the time and the change of watches.

Source A

We drank water that was yellow and stinking. We had to use sawdust for food, and some of us could not get enough of the rats to eat.

Antonio Pigafetta, who sailed round the world with Magellan, wrote about what happened when they had been at sea for nearly four months.

Source B

This is a modern drawing of a ship in the 1500s. The wooden sides have not been drawn, so that you can see inside the ship.

The job of each watch was to run the ship and to do routine cleaning, mending and repairing. Sailors on watch pumped out sea water, adjusted sails, scrubbed decks, checked the cargo and mended sails and ropes. Some sailors were look-outs. They stood in the **crow's nest** at the top of the mast and shouted out if they saw land, another ship, or any sort of danger. One of the ship's **officers** would then tell the **helmsman**, who was steering the ship with the **tiller**, to change course.

Source C

It rotted all my gums. I cut away the dead flesh and caused much blood to flow. I rinsed my mouth and teeth with urine, rubbing them very hard. I could not eat. I wanted to swallow but could not chew.

A 15th-century sailor describes what it was like to have scurvy.

Scurvy

Scurvy is not a disease you catch, like measles. It is a condition you develop. Source C tells you what one sailor in the 1400s felt like when he developed scurvy.

Anyone can develop scurvy. Scurvy makes people's gums bleed; horrible boils grow on their bodies and their arms and legs ache terribly. It takes a long time to die from scurvy. It gradually makes a person weaker and weaker.

In the 15th and 16th centuries many ships were wrecked because they were sailed by sailors who were too weak from scurvy to know what they were doing.

We now know scurvy is caused by lack of vitamin C. Although vitamins were not discovered until the 20th century, before then many ships' captains had realized that scurvy was caused by the lack of vegetables and fresh fruit. Captains took on board as much as they could before each voyage, as well as fresh lemons and limes.

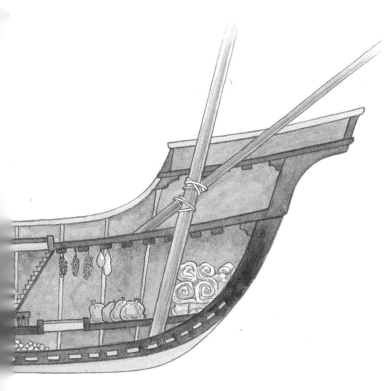

4.4 How do we know? The *Mary Rose*

The only picture of the *Mary Rose* to survive from the 1500s.

It was 1545. A French fleet was sailing up the English Channel to attack the British navy. King Henry VIII stood watching his ships sail slowly out of Portsmouth harbour to attack. The ships were led by the *Henry Grace à Dieu*, which everyone called 'Great Harry', and the *Mary Rose*. They were the biggest ships in the navy. A few years earlier thay had both been rebuilt. **Gun ports** had been cut in their sides and their guns moved down below the deck. Now they could fire **broadsides** at the enemy. The two fleets moved together, gun ports open, guns at the ready. Suddenly the *Mary Rose* tipped over and slowly sank.

Why had this happened? There were 700 people on board instead of the usual 415. This made the ship difficult to manage. Then the sails were put up badly, and the ship tipped to one side. The sea poured in through the open gun ports. Sailors, archers, pikemen and servants drowned. So did the vice-Admiral, Sir George Carew. Only 35 people survived. No one knew know how to raise the ship. The *Mary Rose*, a fully equipped fighting ship of the 1540s, sank deeper and deeper into soft sand and mud outside Portsmouth harbour.

Archaeologists began working underwater on the *Mary Rose* in 1967. What they found tells us a lot about ships in the 1500s. Everything from the *Mary Rose* was brought to the surface, cleaned, labelled and photographed. In 1982 archaeologists and engineers brought the wooden hull up to the surface.

Source D

An archaeologist makes a sketch of a piece of leather which has been brought up from the sea.

Source B

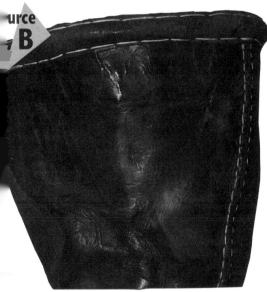

A leather bucket.

Source E

Source C

A leather shoe. Some shoes were found with foot bones in them.

Gold coins, called angel-nobles.

Source F

Source G

A wooden comb in a leather case.

Bowls, jars, a drug flask and a syringe.

How do we know about the past?

Sources A–G all tell us something about the past. We know, for example, that some people in the 1500s wore leather shoes and that the *Mary Rose* was equipped with leather buckets. We do not know, just from these sources, whether it was usual for people on ships to wear leather shoes, or whether leather buckets were common. We would have to look at the evidence from far more ships before we could be sure.

The items from the *Mary Rose* were all brought to the surface by archaeologists who had been specially trained to work underwater. Objects that are recovered from the sea need special treatment. When they were under the sea they became impregnated with salts and attacked by underwater creatures such as tiny worms and molluscs. Once the objects are out of the sea and in the air they change almost instantly. They have to be specially treated.

Articles made of wood and leather were put in special freeze dryers to take out the water. Cloth and rope were put in streams of fresh water to wash out the salts and other impurities. Archaeologists bring objects to the surface. Conservationists make sure they are not lost for ever.

A modern painting showing life aboard the *Mary Rose*.

4.5 The Spanish Armada 1588

King Philip II of Spain wanted to invade England. He ordered a vast fleet of ships to gather in Cadiz harbour. They were to sail for England. Their commander, the Duke of Medina Sidonia, had orders to sail up the English Channel and collect troops from the Netherlands. These troops would be used to invade England.

The Spanish Armada was seen off the coast of Cornwall on 19 July 1588. The ships were sailing close together in a great crescent shape. The strongest ships were on the outside. The English fleet set out from Plymouth after them. The English ships were the same length as the Spanish ships, but the newer ones were not so high in the water. This made them quicker and easier to manoeuvre.

The Armada moved slowly along the English Channel. The English ships attacked when they could, but did no real damage. After nine days the Armada anchored off Calais. It was then the English used fireships. Eight old ships were stuffed full with anything that would burn. Their cannons were loaded and the ships were set alight. They sailed, with no one aboard, straight into the Spanish fleet. There was enormous confusion. The Spanish ships scattered. Then the English attacked. By the end of the day, 800 Spaniards were dead, 3 Spanish ships were sunk and many more badly damaged. The English lost only 50 men and no ships.

Source A

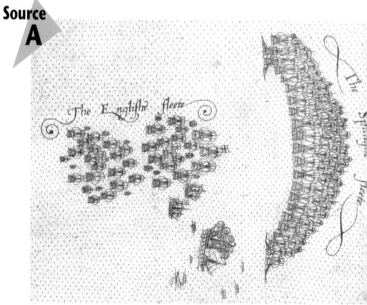

The English fleet

The Spanish fleet

This is part of a chart. It shows the Armada sailing up the English Channel in 1588. It was made by an Englishman, Robert Adams, shortly afterwards.

Source B

The ships were 64 in number, being of a huge size and very stately built and so high they looked like great castles.

An Englishman describes what he saw when he looked at the Armada.

Source C

We could little depend upon the ships that remained, the English fleet being so superior to ours in this sort of fighting because of the strength of their artillery [guns] and the fast sailing of their ships.

Part of a letter from Medina Sidonia, the Spanish commander, to his king, Philip II of Spain.

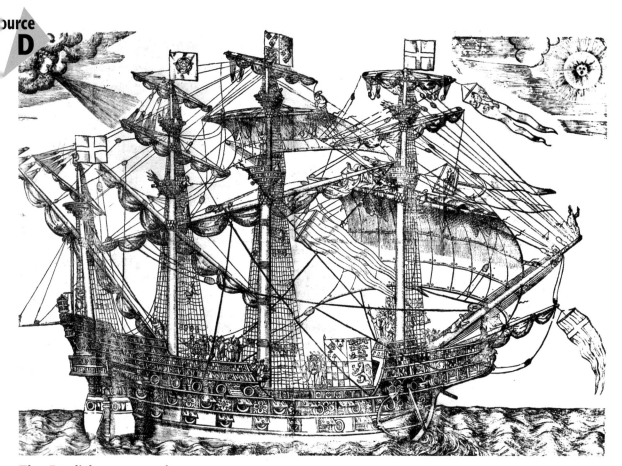

The English commander was Lord Howard of Effingham. This picture of his flagship, the *Ark Royal*, was drawn at the time. The ship was new in 1588.

The Armada limped home to Spain. The ships were blown north, around the coast of Scotland, and then south past Ireland. Many ships were wrecked in the terrible winter storms. Altogether 51 ships were lost and 20,000 men killed.

Tilbury

On 29 July 1588 English soldiers were gathered at Tilbury, by the River Thames outside London. They were ready to board ship to fight the Spanish Armada. Queen Elizabeth I spoke to them. She was sitting on a horse, and was wearing a breastplate and carrying a sword. This is part of what she said to the soldiers:

'I know I have the body of a weak and feeble woman, but I have the heart and stomach of a king, and a king of England, too; and think foul scorn that Parma, or Spain, or any prince of Europe, should dare to invade the borders of my realm.'

4.6 The slave trade

At the beginning of the 1500s, Spanish and Portuguese merchants began shipping black Africans from Africa to America. Once in America, the Africans were made to work as slaves in the sugar, tea and cotton **plantations** on Caribbean islands and in North America. By the 1700s, British merchants did most of the slave trading. Many slave traders became very rich.

Source A

TO BE SOLD on board the Ship *Bance-Island*, on tuesday the 6th of *May* next, at *Ashley-Ferry*; a choice cargo of about 250 fine healthy NEGROES, just arrived from the Windward & Rice Coast. —The utmost care has already been taken, and shall be continued, to keep them free from the least danger of being infected with the SMALL-POX, no boat having been on board, and all other communication with people from *Charles-Town* prevented.
Austin, Laurens, & Appleby.

N. B. Full one Half of the above Negroes have had the SMALL-POX in their own Country.

A 17th-century poster telling people about a newly-arrived cargo of slaves for sale.

Source B

A modern painting of a slave ship.

In the 1700s large sailing ships set out for Africa from west coast ports like Bristol, Liverpool and Glasgow. They carried cloth, guns, rum and cheap jewellery. They sailed to **trading posts** on the African coast. They gave the goods they carried to African rulers in exchange for black slaves. Sometimes these slaves were criminals; sometimes they were prisoners from a tribal war; sometimes they were innocent people who had been captured for the slave trade. Ships full of slaves sailed across the Atlantic to the West Indies and America. Many slaves died on the journey. Those who survived were sold to plantation owners. The ships were then loaded with cotton, sugar and tobacco before sailing back to Britain. The whole round trip took between nine months and a year.

Abolition!

In 1787 the Society for the Abolition of the Slave Trade was formed in Britain. Many important and influential people supported it. They persuaded Parliament that the trade in slaves had to be stopped. In 1807 Parliament made it an offence for any British subject to take part in the capture and transport of slaves.

The next step was to set free all slaves working in the British Empire. In 1833 slavery was abolished throughout the British Empire. The government paid the former slave owners a total of £20 million – £37 per slave.

4.7 The Battle of Trafalgar 1805

Napoleon Bonaparte, the ruler of France, tried to take over Europe at the beginning of the 1800s. One of Napoleon's problems was that the British navy was the most powerful in the world. This meant that he couldn't move soldiers and supplies by sea without risking a battle. He couldn't invade Britain until he destroyed the British navy.

For eighteen months the British Mediterranean fleet, commanded by Lord Nelson, had kept the French navy trapped in Toulon harbour. In March 1805 the French ships managed to slip away and joined up with the Spanish navy. Nelson chased them. He finally caught up with them on 21 March off Cape Trafalgar, close to Gibraltar. Both sides got ready for a great sea battle.

Source A

A modern photograph of HMS *Victory* at Portsmouth.

Source B

England expects that every man will do his duty.

This message was sent by Lord Nelson to the British fleet at the beginning of the Battle of Trafalgar. The message was in a special code using flags flown from the mast of his ship, HMS *Victory*.

Source C

This diagram shows the position of the most important ships in the British, French and Spanish fleets at the start of the Battle of Trafalgar.

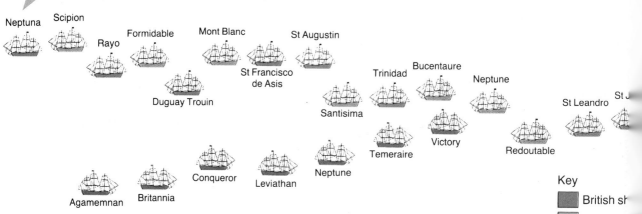

Neptuna Scipion Rayo Formidable Mont Blanc St Augustin

Duguay Trouin St Francisco de Asis

Trinidad Bucentaure Neptune

Santisima

St Leandro St J

Agamemnan Britannia Conqueror Leviathan Neptune Temeraire Victory Redoutable

Key

British sh

French s

Spanish

At the command 'Clear for action', men washed decks down and sprinkled them with sand; they rigged up nets to catch falling masts and rigging; they opened gun ports and made the guns ready for action; they filled buckets of water. In ten minutes the British fleet, led by Nelson in his flagship HMS *Victory*, was ready for battle.

Guns blazed, firing from gun ports in the sides of the ships. Cannon balls screamed through the air; sails, masts and rigging fell in tangled masses; rudders and hulls were smashed. The British could fire and reload in 90 seconds. The French and Spanish took much longer. Marksmen, high up in the rigging, fired muskets and threw grenades. The fighting raged for nearly four hours. When the battle ended 23 of the 34 French and Spanish ships were sunk; over 4,000 of their men were killed and 2,000 were wounded. All 27 British ships were still afloat, but 449 men were dead and over 1,000 wounded. Lord Nelson was dead, killed by a French musket ball.

At the end of the Battle of Trafalgar, the British navy controlled the seas.

A picture of the deck of HMS *Victory* during the Battle of Trafalgar. It was painted by Denis Dighton a few years after the battle.

Nelson

Horatio Nelson was born in Norfolk in 1758. He joined the navy in 1770, and fought in the West Indies, the East Indies, the Mediterranean Sea and the Baltic Sea. In sea battles in 1794 he lost his left eye, and in 1796 his right arm. After the Battle of the Nile (1798) he was made a viscount and given a pension of £2,000 a year by Parliament. At the Battle of Copenhagen (1801) he disobeyed orders and won a great victory. There is a story that he was told not to advance if he saw any enemy ships. So he put his telescope to his blind eye and said, 'I see no ships' – and advanced. Nelson was killed at the Battle of Trafalgar in 1805. Sailors preserved his body in rum whilst the *Victory* sailed for England. Nelson is buried in St Paul's Cathedral, in London.

4.8 Life on board ship: emigrant ships

Between 1800 and 1850 over three million men, women and children left the United Kingdom to begin new lives overseas. They travelled by ship to Canada, the USA, South Africa, Australia and New Zealand. Why did they go?

Thousands were driven out of Scotland because the landlords in the Highlands wanted to use the land for sheep farming. Thousands more were desperate to get away from Ireland because the potato crop had failed and people were dying of starvation. People emigrated from England and Wales because they were desperately poor and thought they would have a better life overseas.

The emigrants' lives depended on the captain and crew. It was their job to sail the ship skilfully, to make sure that the ship was kept clean, and to see that the emigrants had enough good food and water. Some voyages were disastrous. Between 1847 and 1853 over 50 emigrant ships were wrecked. Many emigrants fell ill on the journey. In 1852 there was a government enquiry into the ship *Ticonderoga* because 168 out of its 814 passengers died on the journey to Australia.

Source B

We left Plymouth on 7 February and arrived in Melbourne on 6 June. Philip was sick a day or two; John and Isaac were quite at home; Mary, Eliza and Ellen were very well. We had a very good Captain but a very bad doctor. We had six births and seven deaths. We had plenty of food, but the little girls' teeth were not strong enough to eat the biscuits. The water got very bad. The weather came into a calm and we lay just in one place for three weeks. The sailors caught fish and four sharks. We caught sea birds: they were very good for eating. We had one gale then we got into a cold climate.

Part of a letter written to her father by Mrs Phillips who emigrated to Australia in 1849.

Source A

Hundreds of poor people, men, women and children, of all ages from the drivelling idiot of 90 to the babe just born, huddled together, without light, without air, wallowing in filth, sick in body, dispirited in heart.

Part of a letter home from Stephen de Vere, who sailed with Irish emigrants to Canada in 1847.

The Irish potato famine

About 3 million people in Ireland (about half the population) depended on potatoes as their main food. In the spring of 1845 a dreadful virus spread amongst the potatoes already planted in the soil. When they were dug up, one in three was rotten. This meant famine. Between 1845 and 1848 about 21,000 people died from starvation and one million more from diseases like typhus, cholera and dysentry.

A modern painting of emigrants on board ship in the 19th century.

4.9 Clippers

In 1800 British ships carried more goods than the ships of any other country in the world. Large merchant sailing ships carried goods like wool, tea, coal, sugar, flour and wheat to and from ports in Britain and the rest of the world.

The Americans began building new, fast sailing ships. These ships were designed to cut through the waves instead of riding over them. They were long and narrow, with almost straight sides, flat decks and masses of huge sails. They were called **clippers**. The first American clipper, called the *Ann McKinn*, was built in Baltimore in 1832.

Quickly the British ship owners built clippers too. They did not want the American clippers to take trade away from them. Merchants made a lot of money from trade with India and China, and British ship owners and merchants did not want to lose out. Soon British and American clippers were racing each other along the trade routes to India, China and Australia, with their holds full of tea, wool and the drug opium. In 1865 the *Sir Lancelot*, a British clipper fully laden with tea, took 85 days to sail from Foochow, China, to the Lizard in Cornwall. No ship had done the journey faster.

The End of Clippers

Clippers did not last for long. Some ship builders began to put steam powered engines into the ships they built.

1854 John Elder invented the compound engine. This meant that steamships did not have to carry so much fuel and had more room for cargo.

1869 The Suez Canal was opened. Sailing ships could not use it because of cross-winds and had to go round the Cape of Good Hope to the very south of Africa. This meant that sailing ships had longer journeys to the Far East than steamships, which used the Suez Canal.

1869 The first coast-to-coast railroad was opened in the USA. Goods could be carried by rail from coast to coast instead of having to go by ship around Cape Horn.

1870 Coal depots were set up at Suez, Aden, Singapore and Gibraltar. Steamships carried even less coal than before and had much more room for cargo and passengers.

This picture of the American clipper ship *Antarctic* was painted in 1853.

Were things different then?

Source A on page 14 shows an Arab ship in the 1200s, and Source D on page 25 shows the *Ark Royal*, which was built in 1588. The two ships look very different. The Arab ship was a trading ship and the *Ark Royal* was a warship. Do you think these are the main reasons for the differences?

Source B on page 15 shows a 15th-century caravel, and Source A on page 20 shows the *Mary Rose*. Both are sailing ships. Can you spot any differences between them?

The ships on pages 26, 28, 31 and 32 are all sailing ships, and were all used in the 1800s. Think about what these ships did, and work out whether or not ships do that sort of work today.

5.1 The first steamships

Until the 19th century ships used either wind power (sails) or muscle power (oars) to drive them along. The first ships to be powered by **steam engines** were built in the early 1800s. The steam engines drove large paddle wheels. At first these paddle steamers were used on rivers. Then steamships that could make sea voyages were built. The problem was that for long voyages they had to carry a lot of coal. They had to burn coal to make the steam which drove the engines. This meant that they could not carry much cargo. In 1838 a wooden steamship called the *Great Western* crossed the Atlantic. It used steam power all the way and didn't run out of coal. It was the largest ship ever, and was designed by **I. K. Brunel** and built in Bristol.

The *Great Western* arriving in New York harbour on 23 April 1838.

Brunel built his second ship, the *Great Britain*, from iron. It was faster than the *Great Western* because he fitted it with a **propeller** instead of paddle wheels. The *Great Britain* was the first iron ship in the world to have a propeller. Iron ships were stronger and lighter than wooden ships. Ship-builders used iron plates which were 1.5cm thick instead of wooden timbers which were 38cm thick.

From the 1870s ship builders began building ships from steel. This was even lighter and stronger than iron. Twenty years later they began fitting steam **turbine engines** which drove the ships faster and which used less coal. Steamships could then carry more cargo or passengers.

The first steamships burned coal in their boilers to make the steam. Modern ships burn diesel oil to make steam. Some have turbo-electric engines. In these engines, the turbine doesn't drive the propellers directly. Instead, the power from the turbine is used to make electricity. This electricity is stored in batteries. The batteries power electric motors which turn the propellers.

Brunel

Isambard Kingdom Brunel (1806–59) was a very talented engineer and inventor. He helped to plan the Thames Tunnel. Between 1829 and 1831 he planned the Clifton Suspension Bridge which was finally finished in1864. He built the Hungerford Suspension Bridge (1841–45) over the River Thames at Charing Cross.

In 1833 he was appointed engineer to the Great Western Railway, and built all the bridges, viaducts and tunnels on that line. He worked on the docks of Bristol, Monkwearmouth, Cardiff and Milford Haven.

In 1838 he built a ship, the *Great Western*. This was the first steamship built to cross the Atlantic. In 1845 he designed the *Great Britain*, which was the first ocean screw-steamer. This has been preserved, and you can see it if you visit Bristol.

5.2 Ocean liners

For hundreds of years ships were used for fighting, fishing, exploring and carrying goods. In the 20th century steamships were specially built to take rich people for holidays and on business trips. These ships were called **liners**. They sailed on regular routes, and were owned by shipping companies called Lines. Liners were like floating hotels. They took people on **cruises** to places like the Caribbean, USA, South America and Africa. People stayed on these liners all the time, and only left them to visit strange and exciting places. Some people travelled by liner to get to where they were going to have their holiday. Rich Europeans and Americans had holidays like this mainly before the First World War (1914–18) and in the 1920s and 1930s.

Source A

This poster, printed in the 1930s, is advertising the White Star Line.

White Star Line

Europe to America

For Tickets and all information apply to—
J. BELCHER & SON, 42, Farringdon Street, SWINDO

This picture of the *Titanic* sinking was painted in 1912. People who survived the sinking said that the painting was accurate.

On 10 April 1912, the White Star liner, *Titanic*, left Southampton on her **maiden** voyage. The ship was going to New York with 1,316 passengers and 891 crew. On 14 April the ship's radio operators were told that there was ice in the area. No one thought it was close enough to the *Titanic* to worry about. Just before midnight on 14 April the *Titanic* hit an iceberg. The ship took nearly three hours to sink. There should have been time to save everybody on board. However, the lifeboats only had places for 1,178 people. In the panic and confusion, some lifeboats were never launched, and some were launched only half full. Only 705 people were saved. The rest drowned, trapped in the ship or frozen to death in the sea.

The *Titanic*

In September 1985 the underwater search vehicle, *Argo*, found one of the *Titanic*'s boilers on the Atlantic sea bed. In 1986 a crewed submersible videoed the site and found most of the wreck.

The bow is buried deep in mud; the stern section of the ship is some way away from the bows. The middle part is missing. Most of the wood has been eaten away, but the rest of the ship is in very good condition. There are no plans, however, to raise the *Titanic*.

5.3 The Battle of the Atlantic 1941–43

A photograph of a convoy crossing the Atlantic in 1941.

During the Second World War (1939–45) British and German ships and submarines fought each other, especially in the Atlantic Ocean. The Germans tried to sink ships carrying food and raw materials to Britain. The British tried to keep these ships safe so that they got to British ports with much-needed supplies.

Merchant ships crossed the Atlantic in groups called **convoys**. They were protected by Royal Navy **destroyers** and **corvettes**. German **submarines**, called **U-boats**, attacked convoys. U-boats waited on the surface of the sea. When a U-boat captain saw a convoy, he radioed to other U-boats nearby. The submarines dived and followed the convoy. U-boats usually attacked at night. They fired torpedoes from deep in the sea. The Royal Navy tried to find and destroy U-boats. They destroyed them by dropping **depth charges** which blew the U-boats up. If the U-boats spotted the convoys on the surface, they had time to decide whether to escape or attack.

In March 1943 a pack of 40 U-boats attacked a convoy of 91 ships and sank 21 of them. Only one U-boat was sunk. It looked as if Britain was going to lose the Battle of the Atlantic.

Source B

The only thing that ever really frightened me during the war was the U-boat peril.

Winston Churchill said this after the Second World War. He was the British Prime Minister during the Battle of the Atlantic.

This picture was printed in a newspaper, the *Daily Mirror*, in 1942. The man who drew the cartoon was trying to tell people that they should think twice before wasting petrol which had been brought across the Atlantic.

"The price of petrol has been increased by one penny"—Official

However, one month later things were very different. New, faster ships, called **frigates**, travelled with the convoys. Long-range aircraft protected convoys for the whole of their voyages. A system called **Huff Duff** (High Frequency Direction Finding) could pick up radio signals between U-boats. The British had cracked the secret code used by German High Command when sending messages to the U-boats. In April 1943, 15 U-boats attacked a slow convoy of 42 British ships. Although the Germans sank 12 ships, this time British ships destroyed 7 U-boats. The next month British ships sank over 41 U-boats.

U-boats carried on sinking ships in the Atlantic until the end of the war. But they were never again such a threat as they were in early 1943.

How did things change?

In this book you have looked at four sea battles: the Battle of Salamis in 480 BC (pages 8–9), the Spanish Armada in 1588 (pages 24–5), the Battle of Trafalgar in 1805 (pages 28–9), and the Battle of the Atlantic (1941–43) on these two pages.

The ships that fought at Salamis were powered by oars; those that fought in 1588 and at Trafalgar in 1805 were powered by sails, and those that fought in the Battle of the Atlantic were powered by steam. Think about the other ways in which ships changed between the Battle of Salamis and the Battle of the Atlantic.

5.4 Cargo ships

Cargo ships carry goods to all parts of the world. They carry goods made in factories, like furniture, cars and televisions; they carry food, like butter, beef and bananas; they carry raw materials like wood and cotton.

Source A

Source B

Container ships carry goods which have already been packed into huge metal containers at the factory. The containers are brought to the docks by lorries and trains. There they are quickly loaded into container ships. Some ships can hold 4,000 containers. Not all the containers will go to the same port. They have to be loaded carefully so that the containers which have to be taken off first are at the top.

A photograph of the British oil tanker, *British Progress*.

A modern container ship being loaded with containers.

Some ships are specially built to carry one sort of cargo, like oil or grain, or goods which will go rotten unless they are kept very cold.

The biggest ships in the world are **oil tankers**. They are built with special tanks in their holds to carry crude oil from oil fields to **refineries**. Some oil tankers are 500 metres long and 70 metres wide. They are far too large to get into ordinary ports and harbours. They anchor out at sea and load and unload their cargo by pumping it along pipelines. Liquid gas and liquid chemicals are carried in tankers built like oil tankers.

Bulk carriers transport cargoes like grain, sand, coal or iron ore. These are poured straight into their holds from the dock. Cargoes like sand and grain are unloaded by being sucked up huge pipes. Lumpy cargoes like coal and iron ore are unloaded by mechanical grabs.

Some cargoes, like butter and meat, would go rotten if they were just carried in an ordinary hold. These cargoes are carried in special **refrigerator ships**. The holds of refrigerator ships are specially made so that they can keep the cargo at the correct low temperature.

Shipwreck!

There are problems when bulk carriers, like oil tankers, are shipwrecked. The huge amount of cargo they carry can cause a separate disaster.

In March 1989 the oil tanker *Exxon Valdez* ran aground in the Prince William Sound, Alaska. Rocks gashed a huge hole in the side of the hull. About 10 million gallons of crude oil poured into the sea. The oil polluted thousands of square kilometres of sea. It drifted ashore onto 200 kilometres of coastline. The oil killed thousands and thousands of fish, birds and other sea creatures. It choked the fish. It coated the feathers of sea birds, so that they could not fly or preen themselves. The feathers would not keep out the freezing water, and so they died. People tried to help, but could do little to save them.

5.5 The end of sail?

Tall ships, like this modern sailing ship, are used nowadays as training ships. Young people spend time living and working on them. They learn all about sailing

Although steamships took over from sail for trade, this did not mean that people had no more use for sailing boats. Nowadays most sailing boats are used by people for sport. In the early 1900s, only the very rich could afford to sail. Now there are sailing clubs all over the country beside the sea, or by lakes and reservoirs. Many people join clubs and learn to sail. Some sailing ships are small and easily managed; others need large crews. Some yachts race against each other. The most famous races are the Americas Cup, the Whitbread Round the World race and the Fastnet race. Not everyone races. Most people go to sea in their sailing boats just because they enjoy it.

On 27 August 1966 **Francis Chichester** set out from Plymouth. He planned to sail round the world by himself in his yacht *Gipsy Moth IV*. It was a journey of 28,500 miles. Great crowds cheered when, nine months later, he sailed back into Plymouth harbour. The Queen and Prince Philip sent him a 'welcome home' message, and the Prime Minister, Harold Wilson, sent a telegram. Later the Queen made Francis Chichester a knight. He was then called Sir Francis Chichester.

These yachts are taking part in the Fastnet race in 1991. Most sailing ships today have hulls made out of steel or fibreglass; their sails are made from light, synthetic materials like dacron and nylon.

Chichester

Sir Francis Chichester (1901–72) emigrated to New Zealand in 1919. He worked very hard and became very rich. He learned how to fly planes, and flew alone from Britain to Australia.

In 1953 he began yacht racing, and in 1960 won a yacht race across the Atlantic Ocean. He sailed from Plymouth to New York in 40 days.

Why did things happen?

Nowadays, when people want to cross the sea they can travel in ships powered by turbine engines. These are fast and efficient and very rarely break down. Modern ships can sail in good weather and in bad; they don't need wind power or the power of oars to move them along. Do you find it surprising then, that people still go to sea in sailing ships?

Steamships have changed a lot since the early 1800s. They changed for many reasons. Some of the reasons were:

- the steam engine was invented in the 1700s
- good quality iron was made for the first time in the early 1800s
- Sir Charles Parsons invented the steam turbine in 1884.

Try to work out how these affected the development of steamships. Look back over Units 5.1–5.5. They are all concerned in some way with the development of steam power. Think about the ways in which steam power has affected trade, holidays and war.

6 Whitby: a 19th-century port

This photograph of Boulby Bank was taken at the end of the 1800s. Fishermen kept their nets and ropes on the ground floors of the houses. The floors above were lived in by different families, who paid about 1s 3d (6p) rent a week.

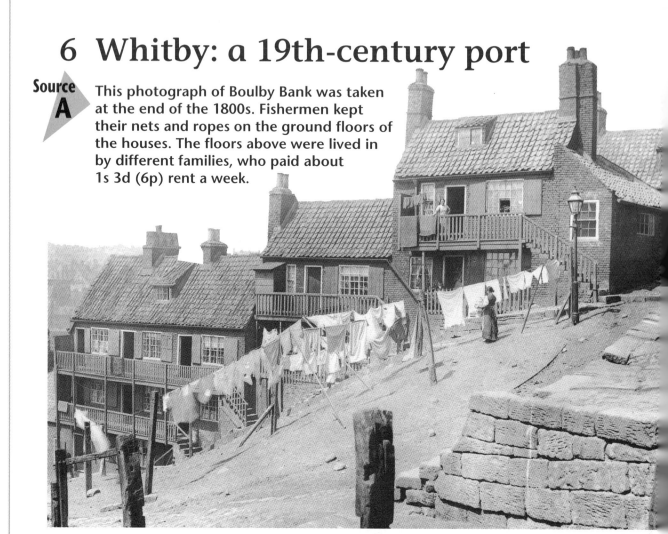

The town

Sailors and fishermen did not spend all their time on ships. They lived in houses, cottages and rented rooms in towns and villages close to the sea. They lived in ports like Whitby. Whitby was a busy, bustling port 100 years ago, with a fishing fleet and ship-building yards.

We know a lot about Whitby at that time because a man called Frank Meadow Sutcliffe took photographs of the town and the people who lived there. He took all of the photographs in this unit.

WANTED, immediately, APPRENTICES to the Millinery and Dressmaking.—Apply to BLAND & WOMPRA, Whitby.

WANTED, an APPRENTICE to the Confectionary Business.—Apply at HESELTON & ANDREW'S, St. Ann's Staith, Whitby.

TO JET WORKERS.
WANTED a steady man as FOREMAN. To a really practical workman good wages will be given.—Apply *Times* Office.

TO BE LET, with immediate possession, a DWELLING-HOUSE, No. 12, Park-terrace, replete with every convenience.—Apply to CORNER & MARR, Wine Merchants, Whitby.

TO BE LET, and may be entered upon immediately, the old Established PUBLIC-HOUSE, *Crown and Anchor*, Church-street.—Apply H. LINTON, East Row Brewery, Whitby.

TO JET-ORNAMENT MANUFACTURERS, &c.
TO be LET, the TENEMENTS and WORK-SHOP situate in Flowergate, and lately occupied as Gas Office, &c, Very suitable for a Jet-Ornament Manufacturer. For particulars, &c., apply to Mr. A. TODD, Gas Office, Baxtergate, Whitby. Immediate possession can be given.

Advertisements from the local newspaper, the *Whitby Times and North Yorkshire Advertiser*, on 7 April 1871.

HAY FOR SALE.
OUT 8 or 9 Tons of first-rate SEED HAY
to dispose of.—Apply to BRAIM & SONS.

R SALE, the brig " MARY BRACK "
294 tons register, shifts without ballast, and carries
ns of coals, or 140 standard of deals, is well found
es.—For particulars apply to Messrs. L ...
TON, Whitby.

NOTICE.
MILIES who wish to VISIT WHITBY
may obtain ELEGANT and COMMODIOUS
INGS by applying to Mrs. BRADLEY (West
odging-House Agent), Pianoforte Warehouse,
Agent and Circulating Library, 25, Skinner-
y.

OBERT ROBINSON,
COACH BUILDER,
ISON BANK, BAGDALE, WHITBY.
ages and Vehicles built and repaired by the
rkmen in a superior style.
class New Dog Cart, Light Cart, Shooting and
arriages for Sale.

Advertisements from the local newspaper, the *Whitby Times and North Yorkshire Advertiser*, on 7 April 1871.

This is a photograph of Whitby Market Place in 1884. Stall-holders paid between 1s 6d (7p) and 2s (10p) each day for their stalls.

This shop is ready for Christmas! The photograph was taken in about 1900.

Sutcliffe

Frank Meadow Sutcliffe (1853–1941) and his family always spent their summer holidays in Whitby. They moved there to live in 1870. Frank's hobby was photography. When his father died in 1871, Frank began taking photographs and selling them in order to make a living.

In the summer he took photographs of Whitby's visitors; in the winter months he photographed Whitby and the surrounding countryside.

Fishing boats in the harbour at Whitby.

Fishermen

Whitby fishermen caught cod, haddock, plaice, halibut, hake, turbot, herring and mackerel in the North Sea. They caught crabs and lobsters too. In the 1700s and early 1800s some Whitby fishermen hunted whales in the seas around Greenland. Whitby became an important whaling port. Factories in Whitby employed many people to turn the blubber (fat) into oil.

Not all Whitby sailors were fishermen. Some sailors worked in cargo boats carrying goods like wool and coal. A man called James Cook learned about sailing in Whitby. In 1768 he was captain of a Whitby-built ship, the *Endeavour*, which was the first European ship to reach Australia.

Two fishermen at the Fish Market Coffee House End, Whitby.

Source H

Fishermen and their crab pots at Whitby. The boy's name is George Walker, and the fisherman on the right is 'Cud' Colley.

Source I

Part of the Cornish fishing fleet moored at Whitby. Every year the Cornish boats caught mackerel and pilchard off the coast of Cornwall, and then sailed north into the Irish Sea for herring. They then went through the Caledonian Canal into the North Sea, and followed the herring south. The Cornish fleet landed lots of herring at Whitby in September and October each year.

Whaling

For hundreds of years people have hunted whales for their meat. In the 18th and 19th centuries whale-hunting grew to be an important industry. American and European whaling boats made long voyages around the world to find and kill as many whales as they could. People in the whaling industry still wanted whales for their meat. They wanted them for their oil, too. Whale oil was burned in oil lamps and used to make soap, candles and cosmetics.

Danger

Going to sea in ships is dangerous. In 1826 Whitby had its first **lifeboat** and lifeboat station. The lifeboatmen had to row their boat through crashing waves and roaring gales to rescue sailors on wrecked ships. In 1861 the lifeboat was called out five times in one day. The lifeboatmen were exhausted. The sixth time they rowed out to sea their boat capsized. They all drowned except Henry Freeman. Twenty years later he was **coxswain** when the men carried their lifeboat overland for six miles through heavy snow drifts. They launched it further up the coast and rescued the crew of a stranded ship.

Source J

A modern lifeboat.

Source K

This is a modern painting of Whitby lifeboatmen rowing to rescue drowning sailors in the 1800s.

This ship was called the *Mary and Agnes*. It was sailing from Newcastle to London with a cargo of scrap iron. On 24 October 1885 it was caught in a gale off Whitby and wrecked.

Fog

Fog has always been a great danger to ships at sea. It hides rocks and sandbanks, lighthouses and other ships. Large ships have in-built fog horns which make a low booming noise. This lets other ships know where they are. Small ships and boats have many different sorts of foghorns. Some can be held in a sailor's hand and work off a cylinder of compressed air.

Fisherwomen

The wives, mothers and sisters of Whitby fishermen didn't go to sea. They worked hard on land. They collected bait; they made and mended nets; they knitted and made lace; they sold fish in the fish market. On top of all this they washed and scrubbed, cooked and cleaned, sewed and mended and did everything they could to look after their families.

Source M

These women are going to gather limpets from the rocks on the beach. They can only go at low tide when the rocks are uncovered. Their husbands, fathers and sons are fishermen. They use the limpets as bait on their fishing lines.

Source N

One of these women is making lace. The other one is knitting a gansey pattern fisherman's sweater. Every fishing port had its own special gansey pattern.

Source O

These women are mending fishing nets.

This is the New Quay fish stall in Whitby. The man with the cap is called Tom Gaines. He fished for herring. Nell Bakehouse is in the middle of the photograph. She is talking to Eleanor Locker.

Ganseys

The woman knitting (Source N) is making a fisherman's sweater in a gansey pattern that is special to Whitby.

Many people say that one of the reasons why each fishing port had its own gansey pattern was a sad one. Sometimes fishing boats sank at sea and fishermen were drowned. Their bodies could be washed up on beaches miles away from their home port. By looking at the gansey pattern, people knew where the fisherman came from and the port authorities could be told.

How do we know about the past?

All the photographs in this Unit tell us a lot about Whitby. They give us information, for example, about what the town looked like, the sort of work people did and about the clothes they wore. However, photographs can also tell us a lot more. These photographs of Whitby tell us, for example, that:

* some Whitby people had the money to buy lots of different sorts of food
* fisherwomen in Whitby did lots of different jobs
* fishing was a dangerous job.

Try to work out which photographs tell you these things.

The sources on pages 44–51 tell you something about life in Whitby in the late 1800s. Some, however, are more useful than others. Which sources are the most useful for understanding what life was like in Whitby in the 1800s?

7 Safe passage: navigation

Viking navigation

There are lots of ways in which ships can be wrecked and seafarers drowned. During a war, enemies deliberately destroyed each other's ships. Sometimes gales and hurricanes drive ships on to rocks or swamp them with huge waves. However, most disasters happen because the ship's crew can't work out exactly where they are. They hit rocks or run aground in unknown waters. The aim of all captains and all seafarers has always been the same: to finish a voyage safely. This is called **safe passage**. Navigation helps seafarers to make sure they have safe passage.

The Vikings knew their coastline and rocky inlets well. They knew where there were hidden rocks and dangerous currents. It was different when they crossed the North Sea to Britain, Iceland and Greenland. They could not see a coastline for many days. How did they find their way across the open sea? No one knows for sure. It is likely that during the day they used the sun to steer by, and at night they used the stars. We know this because the Vikings have left us some clues.

Source A

From Hernar keep sailing west to Hvarf. Sail north of Shetland so you just see it in very clear weather, but south of the Faroes so the sea appears halfway up the mountains. Then south of Iceland so you see the birds and whales from there.

These instructions explain how to get from Norway to Greenland. They are from a Viking book, the Landnamabok.

Source B

This is a modern picture of a Viking boat. The artist used photographs of excavations like Source C on page 13 so that the picture would be as realistic as possible.

Archaeologists found the broken piece of wood (on the right) in a ruined Viking village in Greenland. The archaeologists think it was once part of a bearing dial. They think Viking bearing dials were like the drawing on the left. The dial was marked with compass points. The Vikings used the bearing dial to keep them on course when they were sailing in open seas.

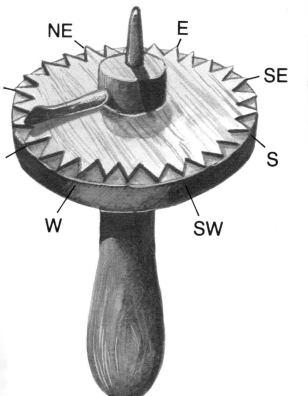

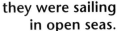

Building a Viking ship

The Vikings were skilled ship builders. They used axes and adzes to cut and shape the long wooden planks from which their longships were made. They didn't use saws at all. Each plank was made with small lugs at the back. The Vikings lashed the frame of the longship to these lugs. They hammered the planks together with iron nails, making sure that the planks overlapped a little.

This type of ship building is called 'clinker' or 'lapstrake'. The other way of making plank boats is to fasten the planks together so that they are edge-to-edge and make a smooth hull.

Navigation in the 1500s

Sailors had to be able to work out where their ship was, and plot a course to bring them safely to where they wanted to be.

Sailors needed to work out how fast their ship was travelling. They tied knots at regular intervals along a piece of rope, and then they tied the rope to a log of wood. They threw the log over the side of the ship. A sailor used a sand glass to time the speed at which the knots ran through his hand. This way sailors could work out how fast they were sailing, and how far. Sailors also needed to know in which direction they were sailing. To do this they used navigational instruments.

Source D

This picture shows a Portuguese navigator using a cross-staff. These helped sailors work out how far north, or south, of the equator they were.

Source E

This compass was used in the 1500s. It showed the helmsman whether he was steering north, south, east or west.

Navigators made charts of the seas and coastlines. These
were very valuable, because the success or failure of a
voyage could depend upon how accurate they were.

ource
F

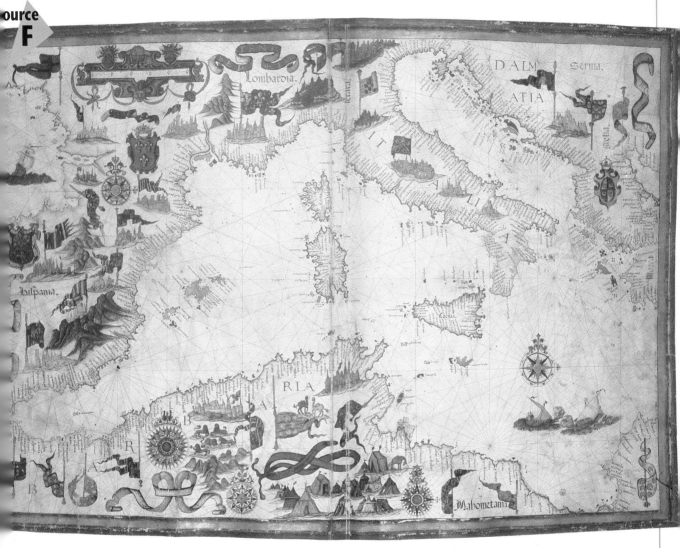

Muslims and navigation

Early Muslims used navigation instruments on land.
Muslims have to pray at certain times each day. They
have to pray facing Mecca, their Holy City. So Muslims
used navigation instruments to work out the time of
day, so they knew when to pray. They used them to
work out the direction of Mecca, so that they would
face the right way.

This map, showing the
coastline of the
Mediterranean Sea, was
made in the 1500s.

Navigation today

Sailors today still need to know exactly where their ship is in the sea. Navigators work out the route their ship is going to take. They use maps and charts and scientific and electronic instruments.

Some navigators use a radio called a **direction finder**. This picks up signals from radio transmitters on land, and records the direction of each signal. The navigator knows where these transmitters are, and so can work out where the ship is.

Some ships can pick up signals from **satellites**. Ships can pick up these signals wherever they are in the world. Navigating officers then work out the exact position of their ship.

Source G

This navigator is using a **sextant.** This measures the angle between the horizon and the sun or a star. He will then use a **chronometer** to tell him the exact time, and a compass to tell him the direction of the sun. He will put all this data together and use special tables to give him the exact position of his ship.

Source H

This navigator is putting his ship's position on a chart.

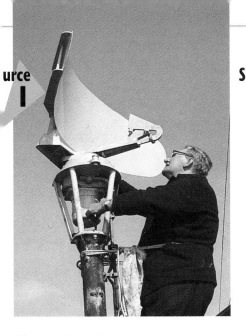

The **radar scanner** goes round and round on top of the mast. It sends out **radio waves**. When the radio waves hit something solid, like a cliff or another ship, they bounce back to the scanner. These waves are changed into signals which can be seen on a screen. The radio officer and the navigation officer can see at once whether there is anything solid within 60km of their ship. In the same way **echo sounders** bounce sound waves down to the sea bed. Navigators can work out how much water there is underneath the ship.

Radio operators

Radio operators take it in turn to be on duty. There are all kinds of ways in which the radio might be needed. The captain may need information, like a satellite weather forecast or the shipping company may want to talk to the captain. If someone is seriously injured or ill, or if there is a fire on board, the radio operator will send for help. The radio operator can also help the ship's crew keep in touch with their families.

How have things changed?

Safe passage is making a journey from one port to another without an accident: to arrive with crew, cargo, passengers and ship safe. Everyone who crosses the seas hopes for safe passage. Navigation aids and instruments help, and have always helped, to make safe passage possible.

The dangers, difficulties and problems which face those who travel in ships have changed very little over time. However, navigational aids have changed a lot. Try to work out which navigational aids, instruments and technology made these possible:
- sailing across open seas
- avoiding rocks and dangerous currents
- working out the ship's speed
- finding out how deep the water is under the ship's hull.

8.1 Pirates

Pirates have sailed the seas of the world ever since the first ships carried cargo. Pirates are sea robbers. They rob ships of the goods they are carrying. Sometimes they steal the ship, too.

Pirates are criminals. From the 1500s to the 1700s, if British pirates were caught and found guilty, they were hanged from Execution Dock at Wapping, London. Their bodies were then chained up along the banks of the River Thames as an awful warning to others. Today, people found guilty of being pirates are sent to prison for a long time.

The best years for pirates were between 1550 and 1750. A sea route to India had been discovered and America was being explored by Europeans. Hundreds of ships sailed the seas to Europe. They were laden with spices, silks, gold, silver and tobacco. What a wonderful opportunity for pirates!

Source A

This picture is of a pirate called Edward Teach. His nickname was 'Blackbeard'. Teach and his pirate crew attacked trading ships off the coast of North America at the beginning of the 1700s. He **smuggled** the stolen goods ashore and sold them.

Source B

This portrait of Francis Drake was painted in the 1500s. He was a special kind of pirate. Queen Elizabeth I knew exactly what he was doing when he attacked Spanish galleons and captured their cargoes of silver, silks and spices. She called him 'My little pirate'. She gave him documents called 'Letters of Marque' which kept him safe from English law. In return Francis Drake had to share everything he captured with the Queen.

Francis Drake and 'Blackbeard' were two very famous pirates. There have been lots of others. In the 1500s Arouj Barbarossa and his brother Khery-ed-Din led pirate gangs from north Africa and Turkey. They were protected by the King of Tunis and shared their booty with him. The Barbarossa brothers attacked European ships sailing in the Mediterranean, including two treasure ships belonging to the Pope.

Bartholomew Roberts seems to have been the most successful pirate ever. He worked in the Caribbean Sea and off the coasts of west Africa and Canada. Between 1720 and 1722 he captured more than 400 ships. He should have ended up very rich indeed, but in 1722 he was shot in the throat during a battle with an English warship and died.

Shap-'ng-Tsai was a Chinese pirate. He controlled a large pirate fleet in the China Sea for many years. In 1849 his fleet was finally cornered by British ships in the Gulf of Tonkin. The pirate fleet was destroyed, but Shap escaped. He was given a pardon by the Chinese authorities.

There were women pirates, too. Anne Bonney and Mary Read joined the crew of a pirate captain, John Rackham. In 1720 their ship was attacked off Jamaica. Anne and Mary were the last pirates left fighting on deck. All the men were dead or hiding below.

Some pirates are made up. You can read about these imaginary pirates in books and comics, or watch them on TV or at the cinema. This picture is on the front of a book about an imaginary pirate called Captain Pugwash. John Ryan wrote the book.

Pirate flags

Pirates in the Caribbean flew flags to tell people who they were. At first they flew a bright red flag, which sailors knew meant 'Prepare to die!' Some pirates began putting a skull and crossbones onto their flags. This meant death. Why is a pirate flag called a 'Jolly Roger'?

8.2 Smugglers

In the 1700s and 1800s the government put taxes (called **duty**) on a lot of goods that were imported into England. They put duty on things like brandy, lace, tobacco and tea. **Smugglers** bought these things in Europe. Then, they brought them secretly into England by ship. They sold them quietly to their customers without charging duty. Anything with a high duty was worth smuggling. The smugglers made a profit, and people paid less than they would have done in the shops. However, smuggling was a crime. The government was cheated out of tax, and customs officers did their best to catch the smugglers. Smuggling is still a crime today.

Often whole villages were involved in smuggling. There was money to be made for everyone. In some places the local solicitor gave the cash to set up the smugglers' gang. In some villages the school teacher kept the smugglers' accounts. Sometimes the vicar helped store the **contraband** (smuggled goods). Can you think how fishermen, stagecoach drivers, shopkeepers and farmworkers could help too? Some smugglers built secret tunnels from farms, inns and churches down to the beach so that they could move the contraband without being seen. They built special hiding places in tombs and pulpits, and made false walls and ceilings in houses. The magistrates were meant to punish smugglers who were caught. Sometimes the magistrates were smugglers themselves.

Source A

The ship *Five Brothers* and the ship's captain, William Masters, were seized by Customs officers. They found, hidden in the bed-places and under the sails, 126 bales containing 3,131 lbs of tobacco and 6 bales of tobacco stems, weighing 178 lbs. Mr Potbury, a Customs officer, told the Court that the duty on the tobacco found in the ship was £1,510 19s. The Captain said he knew to whom he should have delivered the tobacco, but refused to tell their names. All he would say was that they did not live very far away. He was sent to Devon County Goal for nine months.

This is from a report in a newspaper, the *Exeter Flying Post*, on 2 September 1841.

Source B

Andrews the smuggler, brought this night, about 11 o'clock, a bag of Hyson tea, 6 pound in weight. He frightened us a little by whistling under the Parlour window just as we were going to bed. I paid him for the tea at 10s 6d a pound.

Parson Woodforde wrote this in his diary on 29 March 1777. At the time shops sold Hyson tea for 15s a pound.

This picture of smugglers was painted in the 1900s by W. B. Wollen.

When the ship carrying contraband was near the shore, the **spotsman** would check that no customs men were near. Then he would signal to the ship with a lantern or flares. During daytime a different signal would be arranged. At the signal, the contraband would be lowered into small boats and rowed ashore. **Bat-men**, armed with staves and cudgels, guarded the men who unloaded the cargo, just in case customs men were hiding close by. Carts stood ready to take the goods away to a safe hiding place. The contraband was then secretly taken to customers. Sometimes the smugglers took silk and tea in carts, hidden under turfs and logs. Sometimes women smugglers poured brandy into pigs' bladders and hid them under their skirts. Can you think of other ways of making secret deliveries?

Porth Gwarra and Mousehole

Martha Blewitt was murdered in 1792 in the lane between these two Cornish ports. She sold contraband salt. Her murderers were never caught. Porth Gwarra was used by 'gentlemen' smugglers who sailed to Roscoff and brought back brandy. Between 1832 and 1842, 300 tubs of spirit were seized in Mousehole.

Source C

61

8.3 Wreckers

In some places **wreckers** set out to destroy ships and steal cargo. They did not care how many sailors drowned. Wreckers waited until they knew a cargo ship was due to sail close to the shore. They hid and waited for the night. Then they flashed lights at the ship. They tried to trick the ship's captain into thinking the lights showed a safe way into harbour. In this way the wreckers lured ships onto rocks where they broke up. The cargo spilled into the sea and was washed ashore. The wreckers grabbed what they could. Sometimes they robbed the bodies of drowned seamen. Then, like the smugglers, they sold what they had obtained. Wreckers, however, didn't always know what cargo would be washed ashore when they wrecked a ship. They must have had some surprises!

Wreckers

Think about the ways in which wreckers were different from smugglers.

What do people say about the past?

People say different things about smugglers.

Smugglers were wicked. They brought goods like French brandy into England without paying any duties.

B

A

Smugglers were heroes. They wanted to help people.

Are they saying the same things about smugglers?

Try to work out whether these people are saying the same things about smugglers. Do you think that what they are saying is fact, or is it opinion? Think about how you would decide whether something that someone said was a fact or a point of view.

Would you agree that people were always pleased when a smuggler was caught?

INDEX